Hunting Mushrooms

Poems 1978-1987

Bruce Woodcock

木

Avenues Books, Hull

木

Avenues Books, Hull

ISBN-10: 1493797441
ISBN-13: 978-1493797448

For Les

CONTENTS

ACKNOWLEDGMENTS

Some poems appeared in the following publications:
*Stoneferry Review, Bête Noire, Poetry Now: Guardians of the State,
The Assassin's Hour, Delta.*

Hunting Mushrooms

We go through this wood in late October
seeking the secrets hidden from light
we are hunting dreams.

Through this silence, over moss and humus,
over the soft crust of the earth
looking for the rings.

We eat our way through the earth's surface
we eat dreams
that eat the world.

No one knows this is still happening -
the light crumbles, the birches glitter,
the wood is a shell held close to the ear.

Through the dimness, over the leaf mould
we go, looking
for the soft axe that splits the world open.

Cuffley Wood

Roots tangling in their quiet growth,
the creeping moss,
ferns uncurling under old leaves
waiting their moment.
Trees confide, in easy self-assurance
reaching down through the hidden stones,
the dark earth.
It would take a long time to dig so deep.
We keep to the surface, above
the slow upheaval of plant and fungus,
while boughs bend at the wind's direction,
a finger points the way,
a quiet face, an encouraging smile.

Late Night Phone Call

We talk but it all falls short.
A leaf taps on the glass,
and out in the dark someone coughs.
I've been on too long already.
I try telepathy. You sound tired
and draw on a cigarette, unseen signals.
Rain patters, uncertain of its rhythm
and car tyres hiss through the silences.
I say goodbye, lie the receiver
back in its single bed, and go out.
The night that welcomes strangers holds you close
somewhere only a walk across the dark.
A late radio plays through a half-open window
and the trees sway together in the shadows
drawn mutely by the same wind
without a word being said.

Smoke Signals in a Café

At a touch, the meringue crumbled,
its composure shattered.
The smoke from our cigarettes
crept together across the table
and hid among the cups.
What words there were
picked their way like hunters
tracking the rare, the unbelieved-in.

The knife pointed, the flowers hinted
and the white table cloth mouthed dumbly
- nothing else. A bored waitress
left the bill loudly, while we
sat, said nothing, and waited,
camped on our separate hillsides
in strange territory,
diviners, reading the signs.

At the Reading

Across the room you are just
a matter of yards away, though I get
glimpses merely, others intervening. You shift
in a stiff-backed chair, and I can no longer guess
the thoughts from your eyes that steel
and hold no glance too long. Besides,
this is no place for demonstrations -
let the poets do our living for us.

There are facts for how this came about
but at this distance, explaining
needs a quiet language of looks and gestures.
Instead, we have these poems that express
defeats we could have escaped perhaps,
proving through images which plunge and hiss
and harden into meanings, leaving a sense
of something that blurs, and sharpens as it blurs
its point sticking deep, a matter of words.

Hunting Fossils

We search the slate shoreline
for prints of the past,
splitting the soft shale for a sign.

Sometimes there are leaves or teeth,
sometimes bone,
faint negatives fixed through time

to this one place - an enamelled worm,
a ribbed coil mounted in darkness,
waiting for someone to peel open the slate.

Our eyes roam over the broken layers,
losing each other in the rocks, until I see
your eyes on me.

We cleave the moment for shells,
for small lost selves, for clues
to the past miracles.

Portland Stone

Worn to the bone with loving
we go along the cliffs to watch the sea
at the time of the one star
hearing the beat of wave on rock,
caress or blow. The sea blurs
on the round horizon while you stand
in silhouette against the leaking sky,
impassive as stone, giving nothing away,
as the far land eases into the dark.
The coast draws round us like a cloak,
holding its sounds of water and rock
closer and closer to our ears,
always the one against the other.

Durdle Door

Gulls flaking from the chalk cliffs
float in the blue while the sea creams
and rolls – it all still goes on.
Yesterday, appropriately, it rained:
we visited the cottage, house, grave,
and played our parts by the stained stones
thinking as he might on such grey days
of betrayals and life's little ironies.
Now the brilliance of white and blue,
sky and sea, cliffs and gulls,
sharp as each other. You're saying how
he saw an image in the women he loved
as I go for a snapshot and look back
hearing you scream at the water's edge
shocked by the cold, jeans rolled up,
waves sucking your long thin toes
as the pebbles shift in the pull of the backwash,
and behind you, that bone archway,
a pale arm framing a restless sea.

Office Block Poem

Doors closing in the corridors,
the tin percussion of keys,
footsteps swallowed by echoes.

The whole building sounds hollow.
There is movement outside,
there are others, but here

everything is still, behind glass,
an air of the convalescence room,
an invitation just to pass time.

The books listen intently,
the window frames tense,
everything is poised

except for the creak of a chair,
the scrape of a nail across paper, the faint
ticking of an alarm clock in a briefcase.

Come and Go

Jet engines loomed through the summer
that passed into greyness
and the house suddenly empty
but with all the traces
of how we had lived together.
Now I sit in mists
clouds down over the mountains
rain and leaves dripping
no other activity or noise.
I wander room by room
seeking the impressions you made
lingering in the sunken cushions
or caught in webs on empty window frames,
the pane imageless.

Caribbean Idyll

The tropical days seem endless, hot nights
palpably empty. I hug pillows
that make no amends, mosquitos my only contact,
the drone of crickets my only murmurings.
I sink to the sand and burrow deep
hibernating in this winter of sun;
I grip memories, tenacious as a castaway
hoarding salvage, creating from air
what cannot be supplied, bottling messages
to cast into distance, trusting they will home
and light your eyes sometime with a glow
I know lies hidden there across the ocean.
Words fill the spaces absence breeds,
framing moments like exotic butterflies
for you to wonder at, strange fruit whose taste
tests bitterness in each sweet bite
as I sit in the sun of a possible paradise
dreaming of rescue.

Out of My Element

An eager rainstorm breaking this
torpid day leaves mist to curl
into the air and the clouds
lounging like lions on the mountains.
Branches drink the freshness, birds
darting on the grass in anticipation
take off in unexpected flight
into the moment, celebrating the blue.
A plane is shining over the ocean
unlocking the sun with its wings.
I am time's prisoner, imagining release,
encouraging the clock's slow face
to break its bounds so the sweet music
can rise unhindered, each note a crystal
showing things in their own peculiar grace.
The evening unfolds its unbelievable peace
needing no further catalyst; the birds
fan out their feathers, and I cannot tell
whether they are making themselves ready to go
or are already there.

Runaway Bay

I take refuge in a patch of shade
from the sharp whiteness of sand and light.
The keen sun strips my flesh, eager
to see me naked. English to the bone,
I have layers and layers to peel before
I'd reach the ease of these golden bodies
wandering along with only a hat on,
one, absurdly, smoking a pipe,
browning fragile flesh to fullness.
This is the bright side of the island,
the shacks, the garbage-filled streets
seem incomprehensible as driftwood.
The black beach-cleaner who rakes up the weed
tossed onshore by the night seas
digs holes to bury it in the white sand.
He has a withered leg and cadges a cigarette.
The white manager is o.k., he says,
though he lays boys off without warning.
He turns his face when he sees the bathers
his smile setting as he sweeps the sand,
but then religion's always been strong here,
and skins are not shed as easily as clothes.

From the Hillside, Night

A riot downtown - gunfire and tear-gas
the radio says, though from up here
it looks peaceful enough, just the streetlights
trembling in chains which chance has patterned
in the image of a fairground.
Night frogs pipe from separate trees
and the stars are at peace
wheeling together in their random formations
inaudible across a distance which seems
to confirm a balance that has always existed.
In my mind I see you across a dark
that dislocates nothing: for a moment
absence fills and I half expect
you to walk in out of the night
scents of the garden lingering around you
and sit beside me in this darkness,
a star in each eye. Meanwhile Kingston
licks its wounds and gathers in
its brethren, sending its children to sleep
in holes or shacks, to wake to guns,
or gunboats, or just the same long indifference.
The streets are a memory for tomorrow; they gaze up
with an expression I have no hope of reading,
sat here alone on an exposed hillside
and you so distant, the lights say.

No Man Is An Island

Not being a local historian
I remain perfectly ignorant
of events before my arrival.
I keep no records
of my day-to-day whereabouts.
Habituated to the uneventful
I anticipate leaving
without trace one morning
when the earth sees fit
and impetus gives way
to inertia. Meanwhile I eat,
sleep, watch strange fauna,
savouring each moment as I might
bite a fresh russet
or occupy my worn chair.
I expect no more, blessed
with such emptiness;
I answer my own questions,
there being no-one else to impose on.

New House, Empty Sheets

It's the space that unnerves, this distance
between me and my next-door neighbour,
not to mention you, love. You need grit,
a touch of mania and a good rifle
to survive the front room never mind
the stairs; and when the dark comes
haunting the corners, waiting a chance
for a turned back or a dropped guard,
it's a battle of nerves wondering if
I'll get to sleep in one piece or,
an empty sheet, fall prey to the lonelies.

Paper Moon

I don't miss the curtains
except when the moon comes
shaking its fist at the window.
Then the trees stare
at the blatant shamelessness of it,
open-mouthed like children
at a magic show. Meanwhile,
the earth, the stars
rotate like dust
swept into an envelope
and posted second class
for an unknown destination.

What's Knocking?

What's knocking
in the Chinese lantern,
a moth
or a mouse through the ceiling?
The black windows give nothing away.
On the quilt
each flower has an eye-ball.
Behind the wall
something sounds liquid
something's scratching at the woodwork
something pads up the outhouse roof
while the distance lifts with waves of applause
and from the shelf, uncalled-for,
Eeyore falls to the floor.

Double Agents

Each year camouflaged
as root or mould
they wait their call,
émigrés from the dying ground.
At first they take shape
from anything at hand
pebbles, acorns,
whatever is smooth
or moist, or malleable
apparently insignificant
easily overlooked
until the eye picks one
then two, five, ten,
a sudden circle
as they press and multiply
crossing the frontiers
at the flick of a switch
revealing the world's
prismatic dissidence.
And soon
a spider's thread glitters
evasive as language,
while in the far and milky air
a cathedral sails
on the sun-lit horizon.

No Consequences

1

Voices in the trees
and leaves whispering
a hissing like water
and laughter occasionally
a summer evening
with no more to it
than an outburst of singing
or a sudden rainshower
the offhandedness of it
like a remark in passing
that someone might easily
make too much of.

2

The garden is littered
with bronze medallions
in the slow sun
the cats yowl quietly
near sleep on still walls
the wind shakes
the world lazily
and it snows gold.

3

The rain's stopped
water beads
the spindly pear-tree
with points of light
a blackbird
squawks off across the garden
a respite
a clearing up.

4

Pen strokes, or brush
thinning out the clouds
birds angling at a tilt
behind black latticework
or waiting for what
the weather might bring,
sun yellowing the horizon
a sea in the distance
and a cold wait
till it comes back again.

5

A siren wail
among the trees
startles something
in the collected comfort
of the ordinary leaves
until I realise
what it is.

6

What significance this has
arises from ordinariness
the sudden flowering
of a spindly cactus
static all winter
a shape revealed
by a deft chisel.

7

Across the way, behind the trees
an electric saw
moans like a whale
How deceptive can things get?
It just shows
you need to see
with your own eyes
and even then you may not believe it.

Fresh Delivery

Children are playing outside -
the snow, just for them!
Sat at a glass table
on my lap a black cat
oozes contentment
at this white surprise
left on the doorstep
with the morning's milk.

At A Standstill

Leaving the room to answer the phone
work at a standstill
through the window I see
two black cats
one on the sloping outhouse roof
the other in the overgrown garden
benignly staring each other out
given the distance and leisure
of the early Autumn sunlight.
I arrange to give a talk
wonder what shopping needs doing
try to contact a friend
ease my bowels of a sudden pressure
and make another coffee
to take back to the typewriter.
Mind at a standstill
when I return, for some reason
it's a shock to find them
both gone.
Did I miss much in the meantime?

St Andrews Shore

While dawn is teeming in the sea
and dark gulls feed at the water's edge
an old jogger in a paunchy jump suit
slouches like an unshelled snail
along the sea wall on the look-out for health
a reconstituted body and maybe his otherness.
Everything proclaims its unalloyed existence,
pools brimming with colour, burnished rocks
and thoughtless birds, that lone fisherman
checking his pots for what might otherwise
pass unnoticed. The birds lift like buoys
as waves curl and skim in unheeding;
oystercatchers sound out the sand
probing like mad acupuncturists;
spoon-bills with metal detectors scan for gold
and gulls scavenge like poets
frantic for images, to strike the one
replete phrase of the morning and then
back for breakfast with a clear conscience.
The long beach stretches, the wind yawns
in blasé disregard for its direction
and over the sand the tide searches
like a child fingering its mother's face.

Rude Awakening

The sea grazing the shoreline
the wind chasing paper for its curlers
and a jet fighter from the North Sea defence line
screams through a widening tunnel of noise
into the deep. The burn heals
almost blending with the placid blue
while the sleepy onlookers watch open-mouthed
stunned by the mindless drone of the ocean
wondering whose fault all this is.

Seaside Song

The sun is warm, the sea is calm
     the mist won't spoil our view
the air can't do us any harm
     it's gentle, clear and blue.

The fat dogs shit, the seagulls spit
     the seaweed pods go crack
the waves roll inwards black and white
     and roll out white and black.

The dark planes cry out of the sky
     as sharp as any dart
their roaring spears scream through our ears
     and stab us in the heart.

The sun is up, the sea is flat
     light hardens on the sand
two ladybirds rest peacefully as
     blisters on your hand.

Wings erect they tense themselves
     to launch into the day
and they are gone, and we are gone
     away, my dear, away.

Watch That Bike: The Brighton Bomb

Joining the main road from a quiet side-street
I stopped beside another cyclist and waited
for a gap in the traffic that bore down on us
ferocious as ravening animals.
"Almost as dangerous as the Tory conference,"
he murmured turning his head as we
watched for an opportunity.
We took a chance, slipping through
between a monolithic juggernaut
and a speeding Metro. "The surprise is
it hasn't happened before. I trust
Mr Norman Tebbitt is now considering
his past behaviour, though somehow I doubt it,"
he said, and rode on, a quiet man,
late middle-age, grey raincoat,
but beneath the mild manner an unspoken
"It serves the bastards right." Later
I read in the paper the government is revoking
health-and-safety regulations for young employees
to create openings "without injury
to the prospects of the economy",
while the nice conscience of the middle class
which deplores violence at any price
is of course incensed by what's been done
to the ministers who act in its name
but who, after all, are only human.

A Party Line

Desperate for a drunken piss, after
berating Mat for his pessimism, I thought
life's too short to be a pessimist,
pulling the chain on a sunken turd:
there's no place for being so hopeless,
faint-hearted, ready to jack it in
at half-cock before the gate's half open;
this's no time for waverers and swayers
with no sense of direction, wets and wild sprayers
who never hit the target no matter
how big, when there's no doubt about it,
given the right conditions and
a real coming together *en masse*,
we could make a big political splash
no matter what the cynics say
about the 'Sun-mentality' of the 'Common Man'.
"You godda believe in people,"
I barracked the queue, staggering back to the fray
struggling with my zip all the way.

State of the Nation

Over the road are the police
in innocuously blue shirts
like disinfected businessmen.
They will sniff out the grass drying in the attic,
spot the pickets still hidden in the coal-house,
and with little sense of occasion and no irony
arrest the cats for loitering.
It's the state of the nation
breathing down your neck like a sweetheart
eager for confessions, alert
to the slightest disorder
like wind breaking with the wrong inflexion.
"It's the public's duty to inform the authorities,"
so Neighbourhood Watch is on the look-out
in case you publish your memoirs.
I'm told by a reliable informant
that they can't yet read the health warnings
on fag packets by satellite;
meanwhile I flinch when I pick up the phone
hearing it click surreptitiously.

Space Invaders

Afghanistan settles on the cold screen,
troops marching, some forwards, some backwards
like formation dancers with machine guns
playing to the gallery, ejaculating smoke
at an impassive camera. "They shoot
anything that moves, and if nothing moves,
they shoot each other." Out in the dark
a bawling car-full of drunken men
careers past the window on a fairground ride
into the city where kids in arcades
know war's the game for a swift profit,
fingers itching for an easy target,
carried away on some hero's mission
until things get dangerous or the machine speaks.
On the t.v. set the troops perform
rituals from the tribal lumber room
while hungry choppers circle and in sign language
Erich Durschmied explains it all to Charles Wheeler.

To the Intellectuals

It is said
Hitler and Mussolini learned much
from reading Bergson, Spengler and Stefan George
despite the fact that full-blown nationalism
did not exactly correspond
to the personal tastes of those eminent gentlemen,
which, if we were honest,
might constitute a serious
discite moniti for us all.

(note: *discite moniti*: from *discido*: 'to cut to pieces'
and *moneo*: 'to warn' - a warning not to separate
things. From Georg Lukács; orig. Virgil, *The Aeneid*, 6,
620)

In the Eyes of the World

Who can believe
the arrogance of the bourgeois man
with money in his pocket
out to make a night of it,
expecting undivided attention
as if he were a celebrity
or worthy of note,
desiring the world
to order itself to his fancies;
and if it does not
how sharply he turns
into a really nasty piece of work,
a dog with distemper.
Someone should point out to him
that to convince his audience
his pretence to gentility
must go a little further
than the make of his shoes
or the name of his tailor
flaunted with aplomb
or the year of his car
in which he feels so grandiose.
Someone really ought
to wipe him from the face of the earth,
the gob of spittle.

To the Young People

O, Young People
with your extravagant enthusiasms
and undiminished expectations
for you each tree will drop its swag of conkers
with one throw of your stick,
the police always stall their cars
as you ride by on mountain-bikes shouting 'Pigs',
and night-clubs never notice
that you are under-age;
and if the inaction appals,
the course ends up a bore,
the social don't pay up on time,
or the night turns out less than divine
as someone throws up on your best coat,
may you still scrawl
in angry neon
undimmed by the let-downs
that life is one-continuous-hell-of-an-event
and not let anyone over thirty say otherwise.

To the Great British Public

O, Great British Public
are the Dark Ages upon us
or does that come later
after a bit of glamour
if we all tighten our belts?
How is it
that the most appalling lies
frauds and blatant inequalities
parade themselves before your eyes
like loathsome medieval vices
while you smile and wave and nod acquaintance
drooling at their bloated forms
cheering loudly and clapping
each malign princely birth?
How come
you are so thoroughly gullible
and hear no other voices
through the media fog?
Has 'Blind Date' addled your brains
or is it simply the authoritarian state
and the general lowering of living standards
that has knocked the stuffing out of you?
As Jacques Cousteau remarked when asked
why he liked being at the bottom,
"'Oo noze?" What's certain
O unrisen Albion
is that unless you awaken pretty soon
from your miasmal slumbers
you'll deserve everything you get
you pigs in a poke.

To the Adolescents

O Vile Adolescents
what can satisfy you
other than good times
late nights
and a lot of money?

Why, now some of us have power
do we find you
so obnoxious?

Did we sell out
or is it
all your problem really?

But do you need
to be so bumptious
don't you ever feel
like peace and quiet
rather than fast cars
speeding
or glueing up your hair?

Can we not sit down together
and talk over our differences
like why your music
sounds so awful?

Young Karl Marx and God Go for Coffee

I met God on the street last Friday;
he was looking worried so I called him over:
"Let's go for coffee and talk" I told him
and he said alright as if I were a lover.

I asked "What's up, you look bloody awful?"
"It's all gone haywire, I can't cope no longer,
these days I can't handle the laws of creation
and I've got flu to add to the problems."

He told me how pissed off he felt with the outcome
of all his arrangements to sort out the future,
that none of the powers-that-be with the money
were anything like what he'd have if we asked him;

he blamed the Devil and all of his cronies,
he blamed old Adam and, even more, Eve,
and then started blaming the mass of the people
as ignorant swine who ought to know better.

I'd got so angry by this time I nearly
told him to fuck off and not play for my pity;
since he was the one they called the Almighty
it's his mess we're living through and bugger the
                                        whinging.

But somehow I just couldn't give him a bollocking,
he looked so pathetic hunched over his coffee
so I lent him a fiver and told him I'd drop round
to see him on Sunday since he's no longer working.

The Charlie Man

I went to see the Charlie Man
the Charlie Man weren't there
so I hung my hat and coat up
and sat down in his chair

I stuck his printer full of gum
and set fire to his bin
pissed in his whiskey decanter
and gobbed some green'ns in

I left foul messages on his fax machine
and made a lot of calls
to Aunt Lil in Australia
and Jimmy down in Wales

I told them all I was doing fine
though things is pretty crap
'cos I'm on the dole with bits of cash-
in-hand to fill the gap

Then I got this call, I had to go
I'd been making lots of noise
complaining of my treatment
on nights out with the boys

So I rifled through his drawers and found
a dossier on me
how I was a listed person
and the fogies were following me

I found his gun and wallet
and a pack of large crow bars
for prizing open pockets
and a big box of cigars

And when the Charlie Man arrived
I was decked out like His Grace
so I shot him in the bollocks
and now I'm in his place

All you blue-eyed boys had better
wake up to the call
if you're looking for promotion
and a plaque up on the wall

Stand the system on its head
and drink the wine bars dry
take all the lunches you can get
the account's up in the sky

Pull the wool over your sister's eyes
and over your brother's too
you'd better make sure you get them
before they all get you

Keep your ideals nice and clean
and always wash your hands
but don't expect to escape scot-free
from all your one-night stands

Make lists of everyone you meet
the colour of their eyes
their religious inclinations
and if they're in disguise

You'll never live but you'll never die
you'll rule on over fools
making sure the stupid bastards play
our game by our rules

But don't mess with what you don't understand
leave Charlie's stuff alone
there's plenty left for creeps like you
enough suckers to go round

So you'd better watch your step my lad
better keep yourself real clean
learn our self-improvement's not
what other people mean

Yes you'd better watch yourself my boy
you might go a long way
if you keep tabs for number one
and play the way we play

But you'd better watch yourself my son
keep the right side of the line
'cos Charlie's breathing down your neck
like he still does down mine.

Recession Ballad

What ails thee, o mohican'd youth,
    alone and palely loitering
with intent, in your ex-army khakis
        by the conservatory in Pearson Park?

"I'm fuckin' skint, I've got no job
        just YTS, then on the dole,
them bleedin' Tories are out to rob
        us lot, and that's not all:

that speed I got was cut with Vim
        gave me a bad head
- if I find the sod I'll do him in
        if it don't do me instead;

and my girlfriend's had a flat-top done
        with make-up like an Aztec mask
and gone off with that college kid
        from Spider's - it'll never last."

He goes, and as he goes it seems
        his fate is all we live and know
since La Belle Dame Sans Merci
        had us in tow.

Because it's the rich that gets the pleasure,
        it's the poor that get's the blame;
it's the same the whole world over,
        but does it have to stay the same?

Against Pessimism

Shelley didn't believe in Autumn
not like John Keats
with his disastrous love of easeful death

and Blake kept producing
his celebrations of awareness
even when things got so bad
they put him on trial
for shouting abuse at the king
in his own backyard

and while the housepainter's thugs
beat up all and sundry
Brecht never lost
his cigar, his sense of humour
and his faith that people
deserved so much better,
are capable of so much better

and Vladimir Mayakovsky
though he put his own eye out
forgetting for a moment
his poem on the sun
and the rising barricades
of poetry and light

knew even in defeat
there's no place for defeatism
when the balance can tip
if we put to the moment
the crow-bar of history.

Photo of Brecht

From the bar-rooms
the surreal voyages and pirates
the whores read with unusual compassion,
through the dark times
of the housepainter and his boys
to a clipped wisdom
you can see in his eyes -
it's in his eyes, you can see it:
amused, indulgent, caring deeply
while the set of the mouth and chin
show how much he's been through
the grit, the determination -
there it is, a human
commitment, a sense of direction
humour outfacing defeat
and disaffection.
What a lesson, what a richness,
what a gift to pass on.

Vladimir Mayakovsky

When the revolutionary sailors
stormed the Winter Palace
they sang like the wind
a couplet by Mayakovsky:
"Guzzle your pineapple, swill your champagne,
your last day has come, bourgeois, never again!"
And there he was,
fusing his voice
with the voice of the people,
while he recast his mind
from lyric to action
and his voice cracked
with the contradictions.
Eventually it killed him
the struggle to turn
words into action
when his drift and desire
was to serenade Lily Brik
or failing that
fall prey to the lonelies.
So when the cold steel eye
looked into his mind at last
was it the final card
of an inveterate gambler,
the hopeless failure
of his latest love affair,
or the ultimate act
of revolutionary defiance
that made him turn martyr
to fate, love and chance
all at once?

Mayakovsky's Suicide

He wanted her to stay
but she had a play to rehearse
being an actress
and, like him, a professional.
Though he cajoled, demanded,
threatened even, she wouldn't give in
but walked out of the room
refusing to play
'a husband's wife'
even for him.
She opened the door
on a history which
he could not join
a revolution
that left him behind.
When she heard the shot
she began to rave and shout
and her knees gave way
but she would not go back.

Mental Blok

Early in life
Alexander Blok
developed his idea;
of the divine Sophia
the shadowy 'She'
the beautiful lady
of his early verses
and he wrote about her
the most magically vague poems
whilst living the most meagre life.
With the 1905 revolution
Blok came down to earth,
even political,
viz. his 'Twelve Wise Men',
while he wooed and won
Lyubov Mendeleeva
in whom he saw incarnate
the divine Sophia
and later married.
By all accounts
it was a disaster
which must say much
about art and life.
Apparently they celebrated
the first anniversary
of the October Revolution
by attending a performance
of 'Mystery-Bouffe',
the significance of which
surely escaped them.

Winning the Arguments

Canvassing for the party
I knocked on a door to be met by
an old fellar who held up a finger
and said "Now just tell me why
the Council's erecting a statue
to that Irish murderer in Queen's gardens?
If they want a statue, let'm
stick it in their own back garden,"
and glared at me, eyes failing,
then slammed the door. Last week
a nuclear plant went up in dust
a mad cowboy gave us all the shits
and this geezer's whittling about a statue;
but then he's no garden.

A Point of Pragmatism
  (for Steve and Keith)

Gone to make an impact on the world
you leave your ladders. I mash more tea,
contemplate the re-pointing, and recall
your careful plans to redesign this house,
rebuild it brick by brick from the bottom,
replace rotten wood with seasoned timber,
not a surface change but a profound
transformation, finished with plaster
smooth as an iced cake. Meanwhile this wall
looms higher by the minute, defying my will
to shore it up, despite all your tips,
and newly-kindled aspirations falter
at the work in just small-scale changes - still,
full of tea and advice, armed with trowel and bolster,
I climb from necessity with mere apprentice skill
copying your practice, and make a start
at raking the rotten mortar from each joint
rather than have no house at all.

A Right Royal Sunday
(for Sean O'Brien)

The usual Hull Sunday, waking late
to banal headlines: "IT'S A BOY!"
Do you ever really wake before
lethargy sets in and you find
you're wandering round the park again,
a numb head seeking nothing more
from nature courtesy of the city council,
not even a splash of red among the trees,
before drifting into the glass conservatory,
the 'indoor park' where the old folks go
to keep warm, pass time, wait for their teas,
stifling yawns at the tanks and cages
where still-brilliant fish and dour birds,
potential leaders of their generations,
mope among weeds or, hunched on a branch,
eye you with glazed indifference
at the stunning lack of anything better.
If history is news that blooms elsewhere
its roots are here in the clingfilm air
of this hothouse, this park, this city
with its sluggish river marking time,
shuffling its coils and waiting for surges.
No doubt you'll hear news of marvellous changes
in the lives of people you used to know
told by a name with a half-remembered face,
or a face with a name you never knew
you bump into sleepwalking your way out.
Sunday's slow infusion - no matter:

you're confident things are being taken care of
somewhere by someone, and the dinner's on,
and the pub open for a swift pint,
or two or three. Like most things
on Sundays, food can be taken lying down.

Short Supply
(for Doug Houston)

Cold tonight, winter closing in
already on the Welsh hills, huddling
against skies which seem to care
less with the years, now openly hostile.
With your family, surviving as you can
in the shell of a small stone house on a hillside,
you're sitting tight, a fire going,
reading your father's war-time diary
from before his ship was sunk. Something
floats in flotillas across a blank page
signalling that perhaps you too
should keep a record of your own
before history takes over.

                    The valleys
witnessed a different war to his:
police and pickets engaged the mind
in unarmed combat with itself
behind the barricades of assent and slogans.
Tomorrow, headlines will turn on
the truth, some minister intern
an industry without trial
and impresarios orchestrate the peace
with drinks spiked the way they like them,
on the house, settling in the dark
to watch their lackeys, carefully rehearsed
to get it just right, vying for the world
twice nightly on T.V., to palliate
the Pentagon, White House, Wall Street,
Downing Street, Fleet Street.

You shut your book
on a bookmark from Land's End, watch
the coal dwindling in the grate, and wonder
if there's time to order more
before the freeze starts. Beside you
a child sleeps in a cot, peacefully
dreaming a future you may never see
but shape with each indecisive action;
in your hands, your father's legacy,
his story, with its last blank pages
to leave your mark on, while along the bay
on quiet cliffs, deserted houses
congregate round a broken chapel
to hear a word that never comes.
Instead, a cold tide is riding in
reaching to the furthest shorelines
with a hunger that is unforgiving
and a drift that is unassuageable,
ready to sweep over the edge, taking
the trees, the rocks, the sands, and all
their teeming, breathing hoards, unless
the displaced stones rise up to stand
together against the faceless ocean
with human names and human hands.

Hibiscus Tea
(for Annette)

It was hardly nectar. Even the milk
curdled at the thought. It had the same effect
on us, though I could see by your face
you meant us to try it. You were saying
"There should be a word for someone like her,
a feminist word, the gob-shite," and we
laughed at the sheer blasphemy of it.
The tea was red as port or claret,
but had a will of its own, sour as old cream.
Perhaps this was the one the men drank
in the days when the women kept the herbs.
You assured us it must be an exception:
camomile and peppermint are pale and green,
to soothe and refresh, and put the body
back in touch with a consciousness
rising from the lore of your sisters,
a story locked in the leaves of history.
What you need now, you say, is
a glass tea-pot to watch the infusions
as the water draws out the tinctures,
releasing the flavours, slow solutions,
a hidden metamorphosis
which will finally seep through
everything, changing all of us.

On the painting 'The Rape of Rosa Velez'
by Sue Coe

She is pinned by her arms and thighs;
one man leers over her
eager for each scrap of fear,
the other, penis like a dagger,
is readying to ram in.
It could be a silent cataclysm
from Goya's *Desastres*,
but this is the war men wage on women.
You can almost hear the thick panting of that bastard
keen as a butcher, or the jeers of the other;
or the silence they left her frozen in
with the torn threads of hope and laughter
that these women are now reweaving
in secret together, intent as lip-readers,
patient as spiders.

[note: Sue Coe's painting was part of the 'Power Plays'
exhibition at Ferens Art Gallery, Hull in 1984 and was subject to
closure by the authorities responsible, who found the work 'too
disturbing' for public viewing, despite the fact that The Indecent
Displays (Control) Act 1981, which prohibits the display of any
indecent matter to the public, exempts exhibitions in art galleries
and museums so long as such works (i.e. 'indecent' works) are
visible only from within the gallery or museum.]

The Cameo Club

She takes him down
to a late-night coffee bar on Hedon Road.
He knows he shouldn't
be there, but goes from some obscure
sense of duty
thinking he's walking her home. His wife
and his two kids
weigh on his mind, and what will happen
when they split,
how will the kids cope, how will he cope.
A boarded frontage,
whispering at the doorway, then inside
to bleary lights,
loud juke-box, coffee raw as bleach
laced with stuff,
something from under the counter,
and he listens
to the girl rambling. He sees no sense
in the future
as arguments ring across the floor
and the drinks fly;
he hears it all repeating from a past
they all share,
the drunken sailors and made-up women
desperate for
someone to anchor to who ups and goes
or lets them down meanly;
and who is this stranger facing him,
her eyes shifting
uneasily, as if somehow he too
weren't to be trusted?

Decline of the Fishing Industry in Hull

When I were a lad
and me dad ran the lorries
we'd go over Hull docks
and pick up a load of fish-meal
and stink all the way back to Donny.
He still says he knows trawler captains
who'd gi'me sacks of fish for nowt.
Mind, last time we come
were twenty year since;
the captains're all out of work, or dead;
the money's gone
and the port's about nackered,
but somehow I haven't the heart to tell him.

The Quester to His Dad

We speak such different languages:
    I learned the language of the book and pen,
you the language of the glove and ring
    though you never wanted to.

I was surprised when I found out
    your father pushed you into it,
that you fought for his expectations
    and to make the money.

I hear the bitterness now when you talk of it
    though as a boy I never realised:
fearful and star-eyed I idealised you both;
    - it takes a long time to fade.

You never pushed me into anything,
    let me go my own way
and never wished your fate on me,
    but how could I escape it?

And the outcome of the ordeal, father,
    is that when I finally found you
I'd already taken your place, and besides,
    we never could understand one another.

Paternity Suit

I remember the day I tried my dad's coat on
- swamped in tweed, I stomped about
in his galleon shoes, feeling so proud
for 6 or 7 I thought I deserved a cigar,
and smoked myself green until he caught me.
And the time he gave me his pipe to try
at 8 or 9, a real privilege,
and his laugh as he watched me turn sheer white
and stopped me with "You've a long way to go yet
young man." But then
how he found me in my room
at 12 or 13, wanking at some nudes,
the remorse as, sick with guilt,
the world collapsed about my ears.
"You apologised to your mother yet?"
he asked unbearable days later
having thrashed it out in the open for once.
"Yes, Dad," I lied to evasive eyes.
"Well, don't be playing with y'self,
y're not a puff, a'yer?"
"No, Dad." "Well, that's alright then,
son," he said and his hand came down,
a heavy assurance on my shoulder.

Night Moves

After their arguments
my mother would come
to sleep with me
in my big double bed.
I would lie petrified,
denounced as a fidget
for my slightest movement,
yet how hot she was;
so I lay sweating cobs
tense as a trap
enduring the hours
for the first dim sign,
the release of light.

Or sometimes my father
would grope his way in
and soon be snoring
flat out and oblivious
hogging the bed
so my only escape
was to take my pillow
down to the bottom
like a deep-sea diver
and sleep upside down
or be squashed by the weight
of his mammoth mountain.

And when I wake breathless
drowning in nightmares
to this day I wonder
who are the women
I drift to or run from,
and who are the men
that tower and fall.

Totem and Taboo

The primal father whose commands we broke
we ate one night - only for a joke
though after we felt lousy, full of guilt.
Well the old guy had it coming to him,
he was such a bastard - we never knew
just who our mother was, and he treated us chronic,
stingy with the allowances, no girls back
while he made us put up with all his women
til we'd had enough. Snoring drunk in bed,
we did for him, took his money and cleared out.
Then the dreams began: his face was etched
in tree bark, his growlings filled the wind.
I got so I couldn't sleep, so I made a plan:
one night I took his club and deerskin,
dressed myself just like him and appeared
to my weasely brothers by the campfire and put
the fear of god in 'em - they bowed and scraped
and looked almost relieved. Since then,
I've ruled unchallenged, more solitary than him,
watching the door each night, sleeping
with my eyes wide open.

Little Hans

One day I journeyed back
though the scenes were unfamiliar, until I saw
a horse in a field and got an eerie feeling
      like waking to a dream.

I remember my father
interrogating me, the same circular questions:
he was sure he had the answer to my nonsense,
      and he wasn't far wrong.

It did him no good though:
he thought it was my mother. I tried to tell him
he was the one, the horse, the big giraffe,
      the one I wanted,

but I couldn't say it,
and he never guessed: he got so fixated
with his talk about my 'widdler' I swear I felt
      he'd cut it off.

So he never heard me,
since he was as put out by me as I was by him,
doctor-father, patient-son, like images
      mirrors make in each other.

He and mother divorced
soon after. He thought she couldn't forgive him
this perverse experiment that fated their love;
            he was wrong about that, too:

            she just felt loss and pity
thinking it was her when all along it was him,
while the old professor made a scandalous reputation
            from getting it all inside out.

Other Places, Other Mountains
(for Anne)

Launched into the blue unknown
on a flight to catch China before it changes,
you're taking fresh bearings on your life,
doing at last what you said you would do,
asking all the big old questions for yourself and
for a woman alone that's a different trip altogether.
It's a real breakthrough for us, too,
which makes us think twice about where we are
and why we stay here: your letters arrive
and brood like aerial messengers
bearing green branches that tell of lands
somewhere beyond the rain-grey skies
of an English summer. Each installment
conjures new scenes and landscapes, promises
words alone can't capture, but as we read,
with every glimpse of the changes around you,
we grow more restless, unclear of our ground,
while you come slowly to a new assurance
as horizons shift, a sense of perspective.
The familiar fades with each page
becoming faint as the print which accompanies
an old Zen poem that says
one is where one always was, and always
will be: the brush shapes ink and space
as light and shade, catching the scene
exactly - from a high mountain,
a vantage-point over old terrain,

a Chinese woman points out the paths she's taken
while behind her, a mist-filled landscape
unfolds with other higher mountains
that are always there, to be climbed, or walked round,
or perhaps, she seems to be saying, simply lived with.

Inanimate Love Poem

A blue single mattress
hangs over next door's outhouse
somebody must have squeezed it
out their window like toothpaste
till it went head first, and lies
a wet sandwich, a drooping dog
gazing longingly at its only mate
a red double with spilled stuffing
halfway down the garden
forlorn among the trees

Back Ache

On the table, surprised by sudden light
daffodils, wide-eyed as night creatures,
yellow faces expectant reflecting
in the black windows, but there are no bees,
only me scavenging the sleep-filled house
for some peace and the right position.

Night Daffodils

Got you - surprised children
raiding the larder
frozen as burglars by sudden torchlight.
All dressed up and nowhere to go,
maybe you'll lose
this extraordinary certitude
when the day arrives
and you examine your achievements,
but as your heads bow
and your faces wrinkle
suddenly the most unlikely
closed-up bud in the jam-jar
will look out on the world
with this same amazed gaze
wide-mouthed and irrepressible
like the dumb finding voices
or the insane sense.

The First Annual Convention of Bob Josephs

I should change my name
get a forged passport
a new birth certificate
just to be there
when, for the first time
they all smile round at each other
with an expression which says
"What the hell are we doing here?"

Fond Farewell

You warmed my face
cleansed my skin
softened the bristles
eased the scraping
brightened the mirror
with playful light
bubbled your music
left me refreshed
a new pin, yet
I pull the plug
that sends you to
the gutter, and
as your protest
drains away
you leave a silent
reproach ringing
in the bowl.

Empty Spaces

All the advice of philosophers
visions of poets
slaps of the masters
good sense of friends
and still the mind
closes behind iced panes
you'd think had melted years ago
into an easy delight
at the immediate sunlight
and wouldn't be returning;
instead, you're calling
across empty fenlands
to receding figures
who seem to be leaving
(though at this distance
it's hard to tell anything)
until, for no other reason
than it occurs to do it,
you smile at some absurdity
or kiss a friend with some meaning
or hearing some music long forgotten
do an inept soft-shoe shuffle
and with a sigh of relief
walk outside to notice
a wilted starling
floating notes like bubbles
into the clear evening.

Nearly September

Nearly September
and the woodlands hissing
as the year turns

Downpours all summer
scraps of sunshine
battered out of existence

Now autumn takes over
whisking the clouds along
stirring the trees up

cold and vigorous
waking the spiritless
ringing the changes

I wake in the dark

I wake in the dark to the sound of owls
on their way home from trawling the night
as the wind lifts and the sky lightens
crumbling to a fine powder
that falls imperceptibly dusting the rooftops
with dawn whiteness, a reminder.

Winter Passing

On the park ghosts are playing football
fading in and out of the wetness.
Today, death seems more real
though no more tangible than the mist,
something you could easily walk into
without noticing, until someone realises
you've disappeared and won't be coming back.

Suddenly the sun

Suddenly the sun
the egg-blue sky
a piano bubbling
swift-skimming birds
and a lazy cat
on a sun-lit ledge
through dirt-jewelled glass
while the scent of lemons
sparkles, and sunlight
lies on the quilted bed
warm as toffee.

Buddha Mural

He lies on a golden dais
curled up as in sleep.
Round him are gathered friends and disciples,
faces contorted in mourning,
some with snakes writhing from their mouths
which you wouldn't expect;
also animals on their knees,
supplicant, or maybe just tired,
ill-proportioned as a child's miniatures,
the elephant a large cow,
the wren not much smaller than a pig;
and among the intense suffering
the trees have congregated unnoticed
rising like columns, their bunching leaves
changing gradually to clouds, on one of which
three figures, a lord fanned by two servants,
are travelling somewhere, while further on,
on another cloud a lone individual
looks back at them over his shoulder,
a quiet smile on his face.

Just Watching

1

No noticeable breeze
but boughs sway
and look, leaves falling

2

Beaten gold
rocking in air
boats on the blue Aegean

3

The rose I sniffed yesterday
pink shells
on damp earth

4

Seeing the trees
rising and falling
why should that seem like news?

5

Scattered on the grass
a windfall
- the scent still lingers

6

Hidden among their firmer friends
a few leaves scuffling inside the magnolia
finally break free and alight at my feet
silent, inquisitive

7

Gold on green
basking on the grass
curling their toes up

8

No leaves or wind
branches curl
in familiar patterns
not seen since Spring
yet there all the time
beneath the spectacle
like the bed of the ocean
something to come back to

9

Ordinary objects
nothing special
just sitting is a miracle

Marc Chagall Flies by the Window

A blue pigeon
I could swear it was blue
flew by the window
escaped from a painting
by Marc Chagall - yes
a simple Chagall
with his airy blue
flying by the window
among still-bare branches
and perching there
tame and lyrical
as a piece of sky

A Loose Frame

After finishing your cigarette
you'll come upstairs
take off your clothes
and we'll lie curled together
as the wind sucks the windows
and the trees clean their teeth
and if we're lucky
one of us will have remembered
to jam some paper in the door.

Market Forces

We've spent six months with
a dead radiator in the kitchen.
It was O.K. in summer
decorative as most stuff in galleries
but with the leaves curling
doors shrinking, windows pressing in
the damn thing hangs there
rusting visibly, thermostat insensible
or pipe blocked, unresponsive to force,
while every plumber we try
fails to arrive or can't fit it in.
The builder across the road
who's threatened to fix our roof on and off
since the gale six weeks ago
just looked up at the sky
rubbed his hands against his face and said
"They're a funny breed plumbers,"
as if that somehow explained everything.

Wilson's Career

The cheap filing cabinet I bought
from a bust finance company sale
had dog-eared files inside,
names yellowing on the labels
- Mrs D. White and J.G. White Decd.
Withernwick Farms, and G. Wilson:
a dodgy character; a stock-exchange whizz-kid,
who made a killing from insider dealing
then disappeared to some tax haven
to soak up the sun, or changed his name
becoming one of the sleek *neuveau riche*
in computerised cars gearing company research
to defence contracts for star wars.
Yes, Wilson made the most of his chances,
had a fine career, was cremated in style,
a superb pine coffin with a bronze name-plate
for a timely launch into the fires of oblivion
to a muzak accompaniment, leaving a plaque
on a park bench somewhere and a contentious will.
His dust might fill his file now and leave
room to spare. Meanwhile, I've painted
the cold blue steel of the cabinet red
to match the waste bin - bright, brash, garish red.

Ars Poetica
(for Doug Houston)

Derelict in the cold Welsh hills
in the blizzard of an unfinished thesis
your pipes have frozen and your wife's left
taking the kids. The bog's solid ice,
so you resort to squatting in the backyard
over a Sainsbury's carrier, kecks round your ankles,
arse bared to the gale's teeth;
then your brother arrives with whiskey
like a St. Bernard for whom it's all in a day's work.

Printed in Great Britain
by Amazon.co.uk, Ltd.,
Marston Gate.